THE
BEATLE
BUMP

Also by Clifton Snider

Poetry

Jesse Comes Back (1976)
Bad Smoke Good Body (1980)
Jesse and His Son (1982)
Edwin: A Character in Poems (1984)
Blood & Bones (1988)
Impervious to Piranhas (1989)
The Age of the Mother (1992)
The Alchemy of Opposites (2000)
Aspens in the Wind (2009)
Moonman: New and Selected Poems (2012)

Fiction

Loud Whisper (2000)
Bare Roots (2001)
Wrestling with Angels: A Tale of Two Brothers (2001)
The Plymouth Papers (2014)

Literary Criticism

*The Stuff That Dreams Are Made On:
A Jungian Interpretation of Literature* (1991)

THE BEATLE BUMP

CLIFTON SNIDER

Los Nietos Press
Downey California 2016

Acknowledgements

Some of the poems in *The Beatle Bump* were first
published, sometimes in different versions, in *Dan River
Review, 1984, Hollywood Post, Mirage, Poetry/LA, Poetry 'N
Prose, Poetry Today, The Connecticut Poetry Review, The
Kindred Spirit,* and *The Maelstrom Review.*

Interior Design: Frank Kearns
Cover Art: Roy Anthony Shabla
Author Photo: Patrick Letrondo

ISBN: 978-0-9984036-0-1

Contents

III

PREFACE

While going through boxes of manuscripts, letters, and other material for One National Gay & Lesbian Archives at the University of Southern California, I came across my unpublished book-length manuscript on the Beatles, which I wrote in the early 1980's after the death of John Lennon. Several of the individual poems were published in magazines or journals, and I am grateful to all the editors, particularly my brother, Merlin Snider, editor of the *Hollywood Post*, and to Michael Hathaway, who published several Beatle poems in *The Kindred Spirit*, as the *Chiron Review* was first called. The late poet, Robert Peters, offered comments on some of the poems. A big thank you to Frank Kearns for publishing this project.

Michael Hathaway wanted to know if I really liked the Beatles, and this is what I told him, in a letter dated 6 December 1982: "As for whether I like the Beatles, the answer is yes, definitely, though my poems . . . see them warts and all, I hope. Although always a Beatles fan (albeit sometimes a closet one), I only became a Beatlemaniac in the last year, regrettably after Lennon's death." Perhaps Michael was puzzled by the irreverent tone of some of my poems, a tone entirely in keeping with what I know of the Beatles, public and private, and especially of John Lennon. Like any archetype, the Beatles had both light and dark sides. I seldom have been one to jump on the band wagon of figures in popular culture. And that was certainly the case with the Beatles. My poems follow the individual Beatles into the 1970's after their breakup and up until Lennon's murder in December 1980 and Yoko Ono's 1981 solo LP, *Season of Glass*. I include a poem dating from my December 1983 trip to England in which I visited various Beatles sites in London, such as EMI Studios on Abbey Road, and in Liverpool. Also included here are songs which are loosely based on the styles/subject matter of various individual Beatles. And I have added a few explanatory notes for the contemporary reader who might want or need them.

Not one to do anything by halves, I accumulated a rather good collection of Beatles records. Among the few LPs I had bought before the Beatles broke up was the Capitol LP, *Yesterday and Today*. One night I read in one of my Beatles books the story of the infamous "Butcher Sleeve," which Capitol ordered destroyed. A few copies, however, had survived under the replacement cover. My partner at the time helped me steam off this cover after I noticed that under it was the Butcher Sleeve. It was like discovering hidden treasure. Indeed, today the Butcher Sleeve is worth anywhere from $3500 to $25,000 (rarebeatles.com).

I haven't been a "Beatlemaniac" since I finished writing poems about the Beatles. I read perhaps twenty to thirty books by and about the Beatles, too many to acknowledge them all here. Of particular importance were Philip Norman's *Shout! The Beatles in Their Generation*, Nicholas Schaffner's *The Beatles Forever*, John Lennon's *In His Own Write* and *A Spaniard in the Works* (the influence of these is evident in my nonsense poems here), and George Harrison's *I Me Mine*. Other sources are noted with the poems when I use direct quotes. For one poem, "To Brian Epstein," I was unable to find the source of my quotes so I reference a website.

I considered updating the book, but decided too much, including the deaths of George Harrison and George Martin, has happened since I finished the original manuscript, around the end of 1983. I have omitted a few poems and revised others without changing my take on the Beatles as an archetypal phenomenon, in the Jungian sense, for people from my generation,—flawed, wildly popular, incredibly talented and influential,—in fact, the greatest rock band of all time. I offer *The Beatle Bump* as both an artifact and a work of art.

TO JOHN LENNON

Did the colors of your dreams bother you?
Were they purple, not
gold or green?
                      Did the world
look different through a toilet seat?

Was it better in a horseshoe stadium
solid with screaming bodies?

Was it better through headphones,
the music preserved on magnetic tape?

You stripped yourself naked.
You hid with Yoko in a bag
to expose yourself,
to complete the circle.

I half believe the words
you repeated to a world
that paused to listen
on a Sunday afternoon
for ten minutes.

LIVERPOOL:
THE "POOL OF LIFE"

(from a dream of C. G. Jung)

Seagulls guard the harbor,
and on the cliff is the city,
spreading out in quarters
(each a center in itself)
from the foursquare city center.

You come dressed in a raincoat,
choking from smoke & dirt.

In the center of the city
is a round pool.
In the middle of the pool
is an island
where the sun shines
on a single magnolia tree
with white blossoms
and tongues of fire
reaching toward the sky.

—from *Memories, Dreams, Reflections,*
by C. G. Jung

The Beatles Before the Beatles

Looking at the early pictures,
I stare at the drummer,
Pete Best,
& his pompadour,
cool and commanding.

Then I flip a page
to stare at Stu Sutcliffe,
bass guitarist,
with hair combed down
& skin sexier than Elvis.

THE CAVERN CLUB

In the middle of the day
masses of teenagers queued up
to step down eighteen paces
into an ex-wine cellar.

They say that girls and boys
fainted from the density
of bodies, smoke & smell
of cheese, meat pies, piss & sweat.

They say the noise was raunchy,
ecstatic, suffocating talk.
They say the sweat from the band
shorted out their guitars.

Still the four of them sang
under arches of old brick:
Ringo: the kid next door,
the little big-nosed clown.

George: the comely, mystic baby.
Paul: the sentimental Mama,
wailing away with his partner,
rude, sensitive, assertive Papa John.

JOHN

Nobody noticed
he had eyebrows like Fagin
and a nose like Captain Hook.

He spread his legs
and yelled
against a scream of throats.

They swarmed to worship him,
to suck him joint by joint,
to rip apart his body,

each particle of mole,
of eye, of ear, of tooth,
of pubic hair.

PAUL

The instamatics, binoculars,
cat-eye glasses,
lenses of every sort
ate him up.

They licked every inch of his face,
lapped the lines of sweat
as he worked himself
into a rock 'n' roll frenzy.

The faces with braces bobbed,
their miniskirted legs stomped,
spread wide to receive

every inch of mop top,
of eyebrow, of amp, of nipple,
of butt, of Beatle boot.

GEORGE

"I love George!"
said the pimple-faced teenybopper
with the pumped up hair & polka dotted blouse.

"I love George!"
said the girl with hot pink & white
patent leather bag & matching pointed pumps.

"I love George!"
said the Homecoming Princess,
the Secretary of Activities,
the Vice-President of the Key Club.

"I love George!"
the baby of the band,
the boy with the biggest guitar,
the thin man,
the long, tall, solid,
slippery, juicy, dark, dark horse.

RINGO

A sickly kid,
he was partial to beards
when he got big
and rings to cover his fingers
and a name to fit his bill.

Had he been tall like the others,
dark-eyed, handsome,
instead of short, blue-eyed, big-nosed,
and vulnerable,
had he held his distance,
had he done anything but be himself,
drumming his best,
the girls might not have
peed in their panties,
cuddled Ringo dolls,
pinned on buttons declaring
"Ringo for President."

His was the ring
that made the band
complete.

A NORTHERN WIFE

(Song)

A Northern man
loves his woman
better than his automobile.

He loves her right,
he loves her tight,
he loves her morning, noon and night.
  Oh, a Northern man (repeat verse one)

And when he's away
swinging with the band,
a Northern wife does what she can.

A good little scouse,
she watches the house,
she keeps it tidy for her man.
  Oh, a Northern man (etc.)

In whatever mood,
she brings up the brood,
she bakes the bread & cooks the food.

And when he is done
with work or with fun,
she waits for him warm as a bun.
  Oh, a Northern man (etc.)

THE HEALING MUSIC

The front row was set apart for them:
the half-wits, the blind, the deaf,
the paralyzed—brought by their grandparents,
their parents, aunts & uncles, sisters & brothers,
to hear the healing music,
to feel it, to touch its makers,

who sang like gods,
slammed the drums,
beat their feet,
plucked their strings,
shook their heads,
screamed the magic.

In the dressing rooms,
the relatives wheeled them in;
they held out their withered hands,
dripping saliva, twisting their heads,
showing the whites of their eyes,
begging for one touch.

All they had was the word,
the word
in the healing music.

THE BEATLE JERK

All tired of groupies & cripples,
Of reporters & wives,
They each showed the other their nipples
And the time of their lives.

"Come on!" said Johnny, pulling his out,
With a leer & a smirk.
In a circle they gathered about
And did the Beatle Jerk.

429 N. 13th St.
Terre Haute, Ind.
June 4, 1964

Univ. College Hosp.
London England
Dearest Ringo,

When I heard about your tonsils I felt so bad!
I just know your gonna be alright.

You look so cute in those stripped p.j.'s If
that doctor hurts you one teenie bit I'll murder
him. Promise! Cuz Ringo, I LUV YOU!!!

It's allways been me & you. No offence to your
pals, but—just between we two—I think Paul's stuck
up, John's a brain (don't get me wrong, he's cute
allright & I love the way he shakes his head, Paul
too), n' George I can't stand! I drew fangs on his
picture.

It's you I LUV! Ringo, you've got more talent
in your little finger than all them others. So—
who's this Maureen girl seeing you in the hospital?
Please tell her for me—for us—I'm your true LUV.
O.K.?

And one more thing—please, please can I have
your tonsils? I promise I'll cherish them 4 ever.
Promise! And you can see 'em any time your in Terre
Haute, Ringo, I LUV YOU!

(And don't marry that hag, you'll be sorry)
LUV U 4 EVER,
Sherry
X X X X X X X X X X X

817 W. Black Road
St. Louis, Mo.
Sept. 1, 1964

United Artists Movie Co.
London, Eng.
Dear Pattie,
    I saw your picture in the paper w/ George and
in their movie too. I wanna tell you one thing—
George is mine. We been together since when he
first came over here, BEFORE the Beatles came, so
LAY OFF ! ! Understand?
    He's mine. You don't mean nothin. Lay off—or
else—that's a promise, no kiddin' ! ! !
                        In <u>dead</u> earnnest,
                        Deena Anne
P.S. I'm serious ! ! !

THE BUTCHER SLEEVE, 1966

I

Each wears a turtle neck
& a white, slightly dirty, butcher smock.

Paul, the sweetest Beatle, is smack
in the middle, smirking
like the others, with mouth wide open
& a headless doll carcass on either shoulder.

Half a set of false teeth rests on his right arm
while his left hand sits delicately,
as on a guitar, on the smudged head
of a doll.
          Standing above Paul,
George holds another severed head
& to the left, John has one in his lap
behind a long chunk of butchered meat & bone.

Other chunks lie on the shoulders of Paul & John,
on the laps of Paul & Ringo,
on John's lapel & in Ringo's pocket.

Every Beatle shows his teeth,
especially George & John.

II

Capitol Records panics, withdraws the cover,
replaces it with a photo of the four tight-lipped,
motley attired, resentful Beatles,
posing around a steamer trunk, disgusted,
having sold their right to have a say.

"D.D.T. KILLS BEATLES"

John Lennon had said the Beatles
were more popular than Jesus.
A devout Christian boy,
my deepest fears were confirmed:
rock music was sinful after all:
blasphemous,
devil-inspired noise,
elemental and thrilling.

Had I seen the faces of the zealots
who built the fires across the Bible Belt,
the same hideous faces one sees
in pictures of lynch mobs,
the same glassy glares,
the self-satisfied grins,—
had I seen them
I might have guessed
what already I sensed,
what John had said:
"Jesus was all right, but
his disciples were thick
and ordinary."

—Title quote is from an anti-Beatles poster in a
photo in *Growing Up With The Beatles*, by Ron
Schaumburg; Lennon quote is from *The Beatles
Forever*, by Nicholas Schaffner.

GEORGE PRACTICES THE SITAR

I

Barefooted, cross-legged,
tripping on acid,
dressed in loose Indian cotton,
George sits alone
in his English estate,
practicing his sitar
to the voice, on tape, of Ravi Shankar.

Two hours pass & he begins to see a vision.
A holy man arises from the dust
where he was buried on a bed of nails.
He rises above the Ganges,
throws holy water at George's face.

II

Oblivious to the pain in his foot
holding up his sitar,
George plucks the strings with vigor.

He hears the beat of a tamboura,
then a tabla & a sarod.
A cacophony becomes harmonious,
taking him far, far away
from the silly questions of the press,
from their cameras,
from the screaming fans
& their jelly beans,
from the heat & grime of India,
from the flies on the lips
of a child with extended belly.

The Beatles record

They don their magical mystery caps.
They descend into the studio, where
they are comfy, instruments in their laps,
guitar picks in hands, drumsticks in the air.
George Martin, mentor cum steno, sits down,
ready to write, perform, or simply wait.
Mama Paul strums his tune to Papa John,
who sings, adding words to the middle eight.
George brings in a tabla and a sitar.
Papa John, Mama Paul, and Ringo
watch indulgent as George plays lead guitar
and sings, overdubbing tracks—then bingo!
They add woodwinds, strings, brass, Moog & bells,
anything—for what they want and what sells.

To Brian Epstein

"We loved him and he was one of us."
—John Lennon

Was selling furniture a bore?
Did the boys give you satisfaction
you never got from acting
or designing dresses and windows?

Was John a wet dream?

Was your fantasy safer
in dry-cleaned hair,
tailored suits & ties,
& polished boots?

"M.B.E.," said George and Paul,
"really stands for 'Mr. Brian Epstein.'"

When you saw your M.B.E.'s
in front of thousands,
screaming & creaming,
you wept openly.

You blushed, you gambled,

cruised rough trade,
pretended to be
what you were not.

You discovered fear
where there was love.

—For the quotes from Lennon, Harrison,
and McCartney, see brianepstein.com.

Brian's Bullfight

His night life
was a bullfight.
He was the bull,
his trick the matador

who spared him
for a price,
the blood streaking his neck.
One August weekend

no matador appeared.
Without a fight,
the bull lay down
and died.

THE MAHARISHI MAHESH YOGI

A little man
with a Mickey Mouse voice,
a scruffy salt & pepper beard,
a robe, beads & sandals,
he looked down on the kingdom of Maya
—the phony physical world of expensive houses,
high fences, padlocked gates—he looked down
from the air above his ashram
in his helicopter.

To be a guru to the rich & renowned
was to invite disappointment,
ridicule.
                He giggled,
as Ringo & Paul departed,
followed by John & George.
The Mararishi Mahesh Yogi giggled,
being privy to a cosmic joke.

THE BALLAD OF CINNAMON LEMMON

Nearbited Cinnamon Dowell
  Did blondie color her hair.
Did puff it up in a helmut
  To make her stiff Yubby care.

And when they slobbed to beddie bye,
  All pissed & hot & dreamy,
No condick did old Yubby bare.
  He made his Cin all creamy.

Then did Cinnamum explode him
  With a tubby stern and stout.
Ol' Yubby put his organ down,
  Said "Let's weddy, twist or shout!"

So weddy they did & Yubby
  He did trub the beaten splash,
Leafing Cinny with the beddie joy,
  Swinging home his pot & cash.

But then ol' Tabiyoko came
  Behind the Seamie Sadie,
And Cin did cling her beddie joy
  And churned into a lady.

HELL'S ANGELS AT APPLE'S CHRISTMAS PARTY, 1968

> *"They may look as though they are going to do you in but are very straight and do good things; so don't fear them or uptight them."*
> —from a memo by George Harrison, 4 December 1968

"What the fuck you mean we haf ta wait?"
demanded Frisco Pete, hulking over John & Yoko,
dressed as Father & Mother Christmas.

"You got the biggest fuckin' turkey
in all fuckin' England in there
& we wanna eat it, man."

"Do you mind," said Alan Smith, music journalist.
"It's Christmas, you know. Children are present."

Billy Tumbleweed answered him
with a single blow to the chin.

Out cold, Alan dropped forward,
knocked the tea out of John's hand,
splattered his glasses.

—Epigraph is from *The Love You Make: An Insider's Story of the Beatles*, by Peter Brown and Steven Gaines.

TWO SURGEONS

"Ho," quoth he, in bedrum glee,
"They pose behind a caper!
All yub & tabiyoko pudding."
"Look there," spoke I. "I see a dinker!

And she, she's drippin' two bassoons!"
"They be stuffed & going steady,"
Quoth he, "to confabulate a bedding.
Methinks they're getting ready."

"Oh bark the birds," spoke I.
"Glisten how they twit, twit, twit.
They barf their stubbies & blow their nubbies.
They spin a cue to shit, shit, shit."

—This poem is inspired by the November 1968 album, *Two Virgins*, John Lennon made with Yoko Ono and by the events of the night they recorded the album. They both appear naked on the cover.

APPLEPECKER

Applepecker had a gut & a barrel
loaded with roiling silver stones,
lined with mellow jello & dive cluck fines,
each of 'em soaked in Coca-Coola, yet
never was the pecker satisfied.

"Beaters!" said he. "I want Golden Beaters,
each & every won fare & freak!
top of the apple heap, up to my
turtle top & palmaide hare!
Yup, Beaters is what I want!"

Klopp! Applepecker kondered Beater Yub.
Lopp! He pecked up Beaters tree & floor.
Egad! Beater Cart did fowl his plants.
Indecent throw, he explunged all
normal apples from the court.

Cold & belly, Applepecker lost his Beaters.
Out, he klept up his gold & a peck of cheaters.

"PAUL IS DEAD"

When he split apart,
like Jayne Mansfield,
his head chopped off in a car,
girls all over the world
had pieces of him:

in Detroit they had his toes,
in New York they got his feet
plus fingers and pieces of leg.

Chicago and Kansas City shared
fingers, hands, and bits of arm.

L.A. possessed his nipples
while San Francisco had his ass.

Tokyo had ribs and shoulders,
Sidney his left ball,
Manila his guts.

Hamburg had his right ball,
Munich his pubic hair,
Paris his dick.

His heart remained in Liverpool.
London kept his brain.

His eyes, ears, nose,—his entire face
resided in Scotland with his wife,
his Aphrodite, his Venus, his best fan,
who helped put Paul McCartney
back together again.

LET IT BE

I

You could measure their faces in feet.
They've done this before, but not on screen.
No more are they dots on a stage
or on a record or a page.
Ringo and George are grown up and handsome.
John, in love, has the glow of a woman.
Paul has buried his face in a beard.
Is it to look butch or merely weird?

II

Nevermind, when they play and sing
they are boys again,
tossing the music around
like a cricket team.
"Right on!" we say.

Businessmen are annoyed.
They send bobbies
to break them up,
make them four again.

—*Apple Rooftop Concert, 1969*

PERFORMING FOR PEACE:
A TREATMENT

Tired of changing the channels on the telly,
John & Yoko announce a campaign for peace.

They plant apple seeds in the rain troughs
at Buckingham Palace.

They send telegrams to world leaders
to announce an exhibition at a fashionable
London gallery: a film "Peck a Penis for Peace."
A white chicken pecks at John's penis:
slowly it becomes erect to Yoko's song, "Air Skin."
On display: a collage of male & female
pubic hair arranged in vagina shape,
a picture of Big Ben in the middle.

John & Yoko fly to Sicily, float in a balloon
for a week. They promise to shave their hair,
give it to the Vatican
if the Mafia would disband.

They fly to Iceland to speak with the President,
perform new songs: "Melting All the Barriers"
and "Don't Worry Julian, Papa's Only Looking
for His Specs in the Grass."

A final event for peace: John & Yoko,
wrapped head to toe in white & black bandages,
stage a Telethon for Peace on their desk at Apple.
For twenty-four hours they stare into the camera;
they stop only for tea and toilet breaks.

Their performances over, they return to the telly
at Tittenhurst Park Estate.

The End

JOHN LENNON'S EROTIC LITHOGRAPHS

He drew the lines quick,
like their relationship, thick,
stringy, imprecise.

Her hat: floppy, stern,
like his trousers, white modern.
The groom and his bride.

Her fingers a door,
she beckons to lips and more,
her legs opened wide.

So her body slops,
as he slithers thru and plops
his penis inside.

John and Yoko breathe,
their flabby bodies yoked, seized
by love, peace, and pride.

PRIMAL SONG (GOTTA GO BACK)

Gotta go back
Gotta go back when I was young
Gotta find out
Gotta find out who was the one

Made me lie
Made me shrink up and wanna die
Made me cold
Made me shrivel, cover the load

Gotta go back
Awoh, Mama, are you the one?
Awoh, made me go back
Awoh, Daddy, look what you have done

Gotta go back
Gotta go back when I was young
Gotta find out
Gotta find out I was the one

Aaaaawwwwooooooh
Aaaaawwwwooooooh

THAT'S ALRIGHT

(Song)

Our love has made my heart so warm,
We've been together all these years,
Together weathered ev'ry storm,
Our love has conquered all our fears.

So that's alright, my baby,
My dear, sweet only one.
Yes, that's alright, sweet lady,
You're Daddy's only one.

Nevermind the pain and sorrow,
The tempest and the troubled sea—
Love will see us through tomorrow,
Together, darlin', you and me.

So that's alright, my baby,
My dear, sweet only one.
Yes, that's alright, sweet lady,
You're Daddy's only one.

To You

(Song)

Because the world is lonely
And my brain gets so uptight,
I turn my eyes to you, Lord,
You make ev'rything alright.

And when the pain is heavy
And my eyes see only blight,
I turn my eyes to you, Lord,
You turn darkness into light!

And all my blues disappear,
Lord, whenever you are near.

I want to share the light, Oh Lord,
To banish sickness from my sight,
I turn my eyes to you, Lord,
You make ev'rything alright.

And all my blues disappear,
Lord, for you are ever near.

STEP INTO MY ROOM

(Song)

Come, step into my room
Boys, and count me in.
Let's chase away the gloom—
Come and let's begin.

The light is growing dim,
My drums are out.
Come on, don't look so grim,
Let's sing and shout!

That's right! We're all together! Wow!
Jammin' makes things bright.
So glad we came together now,
Cuz we're outta sight!

Yeah, step into my room
Boys, and count me in.
We'll chase away the gloom—
Come and let's begin.

ALL YOU NEED IS LOVE

There is the realm of tears, sweat,
sputum, blood, vaginal fluid, semen.

There is the realm of vocal chords,
drums and guitar,
running from door to car,
from drug to drug,
from manager to mystic to shrink.

There are the row house, the bachelor flat,
the town house and the country estate.

There are the cinema, the casino,
the ashram, the race track, the garden,
the farm, the gig, the studio, the partner,
the gallery, the sweetheart, the television.

Most of all there is the mirror,
the human body, naked and divine.

GET LENNON

The Nixon government
punished him for his personality,
probed his peace lyrics,
his primal screams,
gouged him with kilobytes
of government technology,
printouts on his spirit,
inked with acid animus.

PUSSY CATS

Ol' Yubby to the Tubbydoor did pour
  With a fiend called Schmellson,
Dumping bandy glasses all galore
  With a fever like Admoral Nelson.

On tap was Tom & Dick adoin' their tricks.
  Bedown was Yub & Schmell all yelling,
With Yub a kotix on his head for kicks,
  Butt a bar bell all their fun was quelling.

Ol' Yub with feathers fluxed he parried on,
  Said, "Do you no, ol' bitty, whom I be?"
"Yup," said she, "an arse with a kotix on."
  Whereon the bouncer came, said "Follow me."

Aghast at all to seem their capers,
  Ol' Yub & Schmell sent flours to the weightrix,
Attacking their sorries—so said the papers—
  Abscounding an album with all their tricks.

—*Pussy Cats* is the name of an album by
Harry Nilsson produced in 1974 by John
Lennon during his drunken separation from
Yoko Ono in Los Angeles.

ROCK SHOW, 1976

They flap, clap, enfold
& spread like a space age fly
with moody blue beatle wings,
the nuclear family on stage:
papa, mama, eldest son,
big brother & baby
bathed in lavender
smoke & blue-white laser beams.

A myriad of purple-white arms
reach out to the stage.
They flick their lighters & wave.

Paul & Linda wear matching sequins.
Papa Paul, framed in pink & covered
by baggy pants, does not sweat,
nor does Sea Mother Linda,
hide-hipped, bra-less, & harmless
on keyboards. They are
a pure white dove—
no body and a tiny head.

RINGO ON SCREEN

The look of someone famous—
what is it exactly?
Do we want to cuddle him?
Could he be a kid brother?

His mustache and big nose,
a nose of authority,
a nose that knows?

It must be his eyes,
his luminous blue eyes,
eyes that have seen hospital green,
eyes that intoxicate,
eyes that are naked,
eyes like yours or mine.

The Beatle Bump

Let's all do the Beatle Bump.
First we strum a little banjo,
then we wop bop a be bop a lula.

Then we pop a lot of Prellys,
do a little Bonnie, add a Brian,
bump Mister Best & fall into a hole.

Now we please, please ev'rybody:
we pump promoters, we hump
groupies & we plump for the queen.

We listen to the colors
of our movies, we jump
to the beat of a psychedelic band:

man we sure been naughty girls,
dripping up the barefoot clown,
purple sipping, yellow creeping sounds.

So we do the Beatle Bump:
we jump, we stump, we slump,
we sit, we search, we never stop.

We plump our money bags,
we clump our peckers in a pile,
then we separate:

oh stark flabby Beatle prick—
oh moneyed tankard full of shit—
oh hand me the envelope please.

So we do the Beatle Bump
on a sentimental journey,
singing peace in Montreal,

singing Bangla Desh in Madison Square,
Cold Turkey, Back Off Boogaloo,
Wings Over America, Coming Up.

We bump together, hair
down to our toes, we bump apart,
we hump until we're hoarse.

Then we watch the circles round
the bleakness of a dream, plump
the dream is full: we did the Beatle Bump.

"JOHN IS DEAD"

I

A vacant-eyed Jesus freak
lies on his New York hotel bed,
listens to a tape:
"She said, she said . . .
Here Comes the Sun King . . ."

He fondles his penis,
pinches bulges of stomach fat,
frowns, then grins:
a *Día de los Muertos* skull.
"Ha!" he laughs out loud,
turns on the radio.

"Starting Over," — the words
jab & jar. He gets up,
goes to the toilet,
examines his gut & a shot
of piss.

II

He would take his destined place,
besieged by fans,
he would state his views on Christ,
he would calm the troubled kids,
who would love him for what he was.

"Mr. Lennon," he said, dropping
to combat stance.
John Lennon turned his head,
saw the fat man & the gun,
felt the bullets butcher his flesh.

ROCK 'N' ROLL MURDER

In the end
was the beginning:
the brat-mouthed bully
who gave peace a chance
splashed upon the pavement,
lying in the cop car.

Love had become enough.
Now love was gone
like the echo
in a sound studio.

"YOKO PLUS ME"

I

Here's to the Tokyo child
whose parents left her in the care
of servants, who abandoned her
in the middle of World War II.

Here's to the Scarsdale teenager,
the Sarah Lawrence coed
who made it in the avant-garde
and hid with John in a bag.

Here's to the Ocean Child
who found her hand in the snow,
who picked up the shattered glass
piece by piece with no gloves.

Here's to the now,
the vapor, the water, the ice.

II

Plant a chestnut in a privy.

Screw a lightbulb in a socket.

Dance until your shirt is dripping wet.

Breathe.

Slice twenty-seven grapefruit into halves.

Play your favorite record backwards.

III

When she placed his glasses,
splattered with blood,
on the table by a half-filled glass,
she knew the image would provoke,
that art is individual,
compressed and central,
stark, rich, and true.

—"Yoko Plus Me" was the subtitle of an art
show by Yoko Ono, titled "Half-Wind Show,"
at the Lisson Gallery, London (September
1967); it was sponsored by Lennon, who is
the anonymous "Me" in the subtitle. (*The
Ballad of John and Yoko*, by The Editors of
Rolling Stone).

HUNTING BEATLES

"Are you hunting Beatles?"
—a gray-headed lady on the train to
Liverpool

Yes, I've been hunting Beatles for twenty years
from the moment I heard "I Want To Hold Your Hand"
on a car radio.
     I have hunted them
in the ears of pony-headed girls,
in the eyes of cute boys, under the cracks
of Abbey Road, at the portal of EMI Studios.

Now I come to Liverpool.
The Cavern Club has been buried,
spread between two music stores:
moneychangers near the temple.

I take the bus across town,
past the carcass of a church,
thru neighborhoods of row houses,
to middle-class, tree-lined Menlove Avenue.
(Brian must've loved the irony: his
working class hero, John, lived here.)

I turn a corner to Strawberry Field,
where once, a boy tells me,
a man was killed taking pictures
as I am doing now. Colored leaves
clot the driveway, moss on the stones.

Penny Lane, a mere intersection,
a traffic circle with a shelter
in the middle . . . but you know that.

I turn my body full circle,
clicking, clutching, catching
the same bus I took before.

I alight, hear "Pipes of Peace,"
Paul's new song, coming from a record store.
The boys inside speak a scouse brogue.
They tell me what I've come for.

—29 December 1983

Beatlekarma

started in Liverpool
with a twelve-year-old boy
staring into the bathroom mirror
at cosmic eyes, round & complete.

Beatlekarma is hot young sailors
bringing American rock to Liverpool.

It is the Quarrymen doing Motown & Memphis,
the Moondogs doing the Brill Building,
the Silver Beatles doing Meredith Willson
and Lennon-McCartney.

It is fights sparked by gigs,
Stu Sutcliffe's head, smashed
outside the Litherland Town Hall.

It is eight-hour gigs in Hamburg:
leather, cowboy boots, pills, booze,
sex & abstract paintings.

It is a salamander,
its leg cut off.

It is winkle picker shoes,
dolly birds, gear, twigging,
and French letters.

It is hot young sailors in bed
with a handsome young millionaire.

It is ciggies, Scotch & Coke,
& bald men in business suits.

It is looking like a woman,
acting like a man,
behaving like a kid,
being feted like a god.

Especially it is hair:
pumped up, rolled round,
teased & sprayed,
clipped & covering the ears,
unclipped & over the shoulders.

Beatlekarma is a chartered airplane,
its tail splattered with bullet holes,
a target for jealous boyfriends.

It is two slightly porky
songwriters, one mouthy, one cute,
each married to the other,
and two slimmer mates
married to princesses.

Beatlekarma is the smell
of a newly opened record album.
It is burning vinyl & glossy pictures.

It is patchouli oil,
strawberry & frangipani incense,
marijuana, hash, LSD, & meditation.

Beatlekarma is Arthur Fiedler,
Leonard Bernstein, the Supremes,
Stevie Wonder, Earth, Wind & Fire,
Fats Domino, Aretha Franklin,
Joe Cocker, Tina Turner & Rod Stewart.

It is Two Virgins & the Lovely Linda,
Ziggy Stardust, Alice Cooper, Carly Simon,
the Rutles & the Bay City Rollers.

Beatlekarma is a dive into a pool,
a good meal or a good lay.

It is the execution of Adonis,
the planting of him in the ground,
the watching him grow.

About the Author

Clifton Snider, faculty emeritus at Cal State University Long Beach, is the internationally celebrated author of ten books of poetry. A career retrospective of his work, *Moonman: New and Selected Poems*, was published to great acclaim by World Parade Books in 2012. He has published four novels, including his first historical novel, *The Plymouth Papers* (Spout Hill Press, 2014). A Jungian/Queer literary critic, his book, *The Stuff That Dreams Are Made On*, was published in 1991, and he has published hundreds of poems, short stories, reviews, and articles internationally. He pioneered LGBT literary studies at CSULB. His work has been translated into Arabic, French, Spanish, and Russian.

About
LOS NIETOS PRESS

Los Nietos Press is dedicated to the countless generations of people whose lives and labor created the world community that today spreads over the coastal floodplain known simply as Los Angeles.

We take our name from the Los Nietos Spanish land grant that was south and east of the downtown area. Our purpose is to serve local writers so they may share their words with many, in the form of tangible books that can be held and read and passed on. This written art form is one way we realize our common bonds and help each other discover what is meaningful in life.

LOS NIETOS PRESS
www.LosNietosPress.com
LosNietosPress@Gmail.com

www.ingramcontent.com/pod-product-compliance
Lightning Source LLC
Chambersburg PA
CBHW062027040426
42447CB00010B/2171